W9-BWL-559

PowerKids Readers:
Big Cats™
PUMAS

Elizabeth Vogel

The Rosen Publishing Group's
PowerKids Press™
New York

Published in 2002 by The Rosen Publishing Group, Inc.
29 East 21st Street, New York, NY 10010

First Edition

Book Design: Michael Donnellan

Photo Credits: pp. 1, 5, 9, 15 © Gail Shumway/FPG International; p. 7 © Dennis Hallinan/FPG International; p. 11 © Digital Stock; pp. 13, 21 © Lee Kuhn/FPG International; pp. 16, 22 © PhotoDisc; p. 17 © John Lambert/Artville; p. 19 © Joseph Van Os/Image Bank; p. 22 © DigitalVision.

Vogel, Elizabeth.
Pumas / Elizabeth Vogel.
    p. cm. — (Big cats)
ISBN 0-8239-6022-6 (library binding)
1. Puma—Juvenile literature. [1. Puma.] I. Title.
QL737.C23 V64 2002
599.75'24—dc21

                                                00-012986

Manufactured in the United States of America

CONTENTS

A puma is a big cat.
A puma is also called a
mountain lion or cougar.

Pumas have black stripes from their mouths to their eyes.

Pumas have long tails.
Their fur is either dark
brown or red.

Pumas can live on rocky mountains where there is snow.

Pumas cannot roar, but they can make other sounds like whistles or screams.

Pumas use their strong legs to jump high.

Pumas like to eat meat.
Pumas eat
animals like
elk and deer.

17

A baby puma is called a kitten. Mothers make sure puma kittens are safe from other animals.

When puma kittens are old enough, they learn how to hunt from their mothers.

WORDS TO KNOW

deer

elk

kitten

mountain

Here are more books to read about pumas:
Cougar: Lion of the Mountains
(Rookie Read-About Science)
by Allan Fowler
Children's Press

Pumas
by Don Middleton
Rosen Publishing

To learn more about pumas, check out these Web sites:
www.bigcats.com
www.discovery.com
www.mountainlion.org

INDEX

Word Count: 112

Note to Librarians, Teachers, and Parents

PowerKids Readers are specially designed to help emergent and beginning readers build their skills in reading for information. Simple vocabulary and concepts are paired with stunning, detailed images from the natural world around them. Readers will respond to written language by linking meaning with their own everyday experiences and observations. Sentences are short and simple, employing a basic vocabulary of sight words, as well as new words that describe objects or processes that take place in the natural world. Large type, clean design, and photographs corresponding directly to the text all help children to decipher meaning. Features such as a contents page, picture glossary, and index help children to get the most out of PowerKids Readers. They also introduce children to the basic elements of a book, which they will encounter in their future reading experiences. Lists of related books and Web sites encourage kids to explore other sources and to continue the process of learning.